FRONTIER LAND

COWBOYS

OF THE FRONTIER

Charles W. Sundling

ABDO
& Daughters

Visit us at
www.abdopub.com

Published by ABDO Publishing Company, 4940 Viking Drive, Edina, MN 55435.
Copyright ©2000 by Abdo Consulting Group, Inc. International copyrights
reserved in all countries. No part of this book may be reproduced in any form
without written permission from the publisher.

Printed in the United States.

Edited by: Tamara L. Britton
Art Direction: John Hamilton
Contributing Editor: Morgan Hughes

Cover photo: Corbis
Interior photos: Image Club Graphics, pages 1, 3, 5, 10, 11, 20-21, 25, 31, 32
               Corbis, pages 6, 7, 9, 12, 13, 14, 16, 17, 19, 22, 23

Sources: *American Heritage History of the Great West, The.* New York: Ameri-
can Heritage, 1965; Adams, Alexander B. *Sunlight and Storm: The Great
American West.* New York: Putnam and Sons, 1977; Adams, Andy. *The Log of a
Cowboy.* New York: Airmount, 1969; Denhardt, Robert M. *The Horse of the
Americas.* Norman, OK: University of Oklahoma Press, 1975; Dykstra, Robert R.
The Cattle Towns. New York: Alfred A. Knopf, 1968; Hoig, Stan. *The Humor of
the American Cowboy.* Lincoln, NE: University of Nebraska Press, 1958; Jones,
Dave. *Making and Preparing Western Saddles.* New York: Arco Publishing,
1982; Lamar, Howard (editor). *The Reader's Encyclopedia of the Old West.* New
York, 1977; Milner, Clyde A. et. al. (editors). *The Oxford History of the American
West.* New York, 1990; Worcester, Don. *The Chisholm Trail: High Road of the
Cattle Kingdom.* Lincoln, NE: University of Nebraska Press, 1980.

Library of Congress Cataloging–in–Publication Data

Sundling, Charles W.
    Cowboys of the frontier / Charles W. Sundling
        p. cm. — (Frontier land)
    Includes index.
    Summary: A brief introduction to the day-to-day life of cowboys in the
American West.
    ISBN 1-57765-045-X
    1. Cowboys—West (U.S.)—Social life and customs—Juvenile literature. 2.
Cowboys—West (U.S.)—History—Juvenile literature. 3. West (U.S.)—Social life
and customs—Juvenile literature. 4. Ranch life—West (U.S.)—Juvenile litera-
ture. [1. Cowboys—West (U.S.) 2. West (U.S.)—Social life and customs. 3.
Ranch life—West (U.S.)]
I. Title. II. Series: Sundling, Charles W. Frontier land.
F596.S926 2000
978—DC21   98-3454
                                                    CIP
                                                    AC

CONTENTS

SPANISH HORSES AND CATTLE

Cowboys needed two things to do their job: horses and cattle. But at the beginning of America's history, there were neither. It wasn't until Spanish soldiers brought them on their travels from Mexico many years ago that the stage was set for cowboys.

At first, the Spanish brought just a few horses, but soon they brought many more. The horses that the Spanish brought were warhorses, healthy and strong, bred for the hardships of combat. Sometimes the horses ran away. Native Americans also took horses from the Spanish. Eventually, these horses banded together into wild herds that roamed the plains.

People called the wild horses mustangs. They were strong and hardworking, and they didn't need much food or water to live in the harsh American frontier. This made mustangs useful to cowboys.

Cowboys also used quarter horses. These were a different type of horse, a combination of English and Spanish breeds. Quarter horses had strength and balance, and could run fast for short distances.

The Spanish also introduced cattle to America. These cattle were perfect for America's climate. They lived easily in dry areas, and tolerated the brutal cold of winter and the extreme heat of summer. They were big cattle, wild and bad-tempered, and able to defend themselves against predators. Their big horns helped them fight. The tips of the horns could be more than six feet (1.8 m) apart. Because of their horns, they became known as longhorn cattle.

After the Civil War, people back East needed beef. The United States government also needed meat to feed Native Americans. The longhorns' meat was tough, but there were a lot of them in Texas. Cattlemen hired cowboys to move longhorn herds north. In 35 years, cowboys moved 10 million longhorns from Texas to Missouri, Kansas, and Colorado.

Above: *Longhorn cattle grazing. The distance between their horns from tip to tip can exceed six feet (1.8 m).*
Facing page: *A cowboy herds cattle back into the corral.*

STANDING THE GAFF

Cowboys thought of themselves as more than simple farmhands. Farmhands slopped pigs, planted crops, and milked cows. But few farmhands worked with steers that could weigh as much as 1,000 pounds (454 kg). Cowboys worked with big steers, sometimes herding them for hundreds of miles. Cowboys worked hard. In other words, they "stood the gaff."

Many cowboys were Texans. A large number of them had fought for the South in the Civil War. A few fought for the North as well. Some cowboys were sons of English nobles and were college educated. Some were outlaws. Some were preachers' sons. Some were former slaves, and some had owned slaves. Most were between 18 and 28 years old. About one of every three cowboys was either Hispanic or African American.

Many cowboys used nicknames. Edward C. Abbott had the nickname Teddy Blue. Nat Love claimed he was Deadwood Dick. Mesquite Bill, Wyoming Pete, and Lonesome Jensen were other cowboy nicknames.

Whatever their names on the trail, cowboys worked hard and slept little. In good weather and with a good-tempered herd, they could sleep from after supper until it was time for their night watch shift. In bad weather and with a bad-tempered herd, they might not get any sleep at all. To stay awake, sometimes they rubbed tobacco juice in their eyes. They drove the herd for three to four months.

Nat Love was an African American cowboy who was greatly skilled in roping. In 1876 he claimed the name of Deadwood Dick. This photo shows him with his lariat and saddle.

Cattle drives could be boring, yet very dangerous. Two out of three cowboys never went on more than one drive. At the end of a drive, the herd was sold. The cattle could bring anywhere from $8 to $40 per steer. Cowboys were paid about $30 a month for three or four months' work, barely enough for a new hat and boots.

Above: *Roping a stray steer.*
Facing page: *A cowboy races ahead of a stampede.*

GALLUSES, WILD RAGS, AND MULE EARS

Cowboys rode horses, sometimes through thorny brush and tall weeds. They rode in heat, cold, rain, snow, and every kind of weather in between. Cowboys had to wear work clothes that were strong and long lasting.

Cowboys wore "long johns," underwear with long arms and legs. Long johns were usually made of wool. They kept cowboys warm on cold winter nights. They also soaked up sweat, which rotted clothes quickly.

Cowboys wore shirts and pants made of heavy wool, which lasts longer than lightweight wool. While working, cowboys usually did not wear belts. Some wore suspenders, which were also called "galluses."

Long johns.

Some cowboys tied cotton print bandannas around their necks. Bandannas, or "wild rags," protected cowboys' necks from the hot sun. This helped stop sunstroke, a sickness caused by overexposure to the sun. If untreated, sunstroke can cause a person to have a fever, and eventually lose

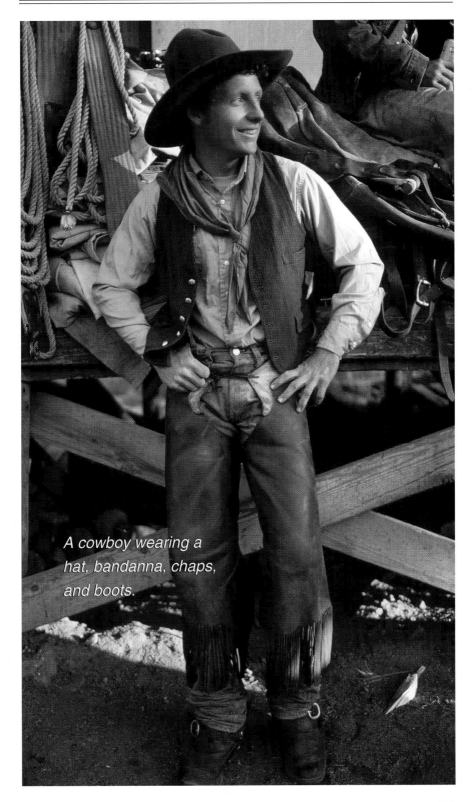

A cowboy wearing a hat, bandanna, chaps, and boots.

A cowboy wearing a hat and tied cotton printed bandanna.

consciousness. Cowboys also used bandannas to wipe sweat from their foreheads. They tied wounds with them. Cowboys also covered their noses and mouths with bandannas to ward off trail dust.

Cowboys thought of their hats as a way of identifying themselves to others. Hats were made from a mixture of wool and fur. This mix made the hats long lasting and strong. Sometimes cowboys used their hats as "quirts," or small whips. They used them to carry water, or as pillows. Cowboys also used their hats to fan fires.

Cowboy hats had many styles, and cowboys wore them for good reasons. A hat's high "crown," or top, kept a cowboy's head cool under the hot summer sun. Its wide rim kept the sun from his eyes and off his neck. In rain and snow a hat was like a small umbrella. It also protected a cowboy's head from low tree branches.

Cowboys often rode through brush that had thorns, which meant that their legs needed strong protection. Leather boots that went from the feet to the knees gave this protection.

Boots were important to cowboys. They wanted hand-made boots that fit their feet properly. Such custom-made boots could cost cowboys $50 a pair, but they were worth it.

Some boots had narrow toes so that they would fit in a stirrup better. The heels of some boots were high and went from wide at the top to thin at the bottom. Sometimes cowboys on foot roped cattle. Boots with high, thin-bottomed heels dug into the ground easily, which helped the cowboys keep their balance.

A cowboy hat rests on a fence post.

Cowboy boots had no laces or buckles. However, boots did not fall from a cowboy's feet because they fit tightly at the arch and against the heel.

Because the boots fit tightly, cowboys stood to put them on. They stepped into the boot and pulled on its pull-straps or "mule ears." With experience, cowboys could put their boots on without hopping around or falling down.

Cowboys had spurs on their boots, which they poked into their horses' sides to get them to run faster or turn quickly. Horses had thick, matted hair. Spurs went through the hair and tapped a horse's skin. Spurs rarely hurt horses—cowboys needed healthy horses, not injured ones.

A cowboy boot, with spur, fitted inside a stirrup.

Cowboys needed to cover their legs with more than their boots and wool pants. Boots did not protect enough of a cowboy's legs, and wool pants ripped easily. For extra protection, cowboys wore leather chaps.

Cowboys spent much time working with ropes and holding their horses' reins. They wore tough buckskin or tanned animal hide gloves to protect their hands. Everything cowboys wore was tough. Everything they wore had a purpose.

WOOD AND WET RAWHIDE

Cowboys could ride their horses 15 or more hours a day. They needed strong, comfortable, and useful saddles. After all, saddles carried the cowboys and all their tools.

Cowboys bought saddles at a saddlery. Generally, a cowboy paid a month's wages for a saddle. This was a lot of money back then, but a good saddle could last 30 years.

Saddles came in many different styles. However, wood served as each saddle's frame. Saddle makers used pine wood that was free of knots. They lacquered the frame several times to keep it from rotting.

Next, saddle makers placed wet leather or rawhide on the lacquered frame. When the leather dried, it kept the frame hard and stiff. Dressed leather was sewn over the rawhide to finish the saddle.

Cowboys roped cattle and hooked the rope around the saddle horn. To make the horns strong, saddle makers made them out of iron.

The shape of a cowboy's saddle was important, since it gave him some comfort. More importantly, the curved shape kept the cowboy in the saddle and on his horse.

When cowboys roped cattle, their saddles needed to stay in place. The saddles had two "girths," or straps, that were tied around the horses bodies to secure the saddle.

A square of leather, or "skirt," spread out from the saddle. The skirt helped distribute weight on the horse and made the cowboy more stable in the saddle. The skirts also had leather rings. Tools were tied to the rings for easy access.

A saddle had to have good stirrups, which cowboys used to rest their feet. Stirrups also helped cowboys get on their horses and stay on them. Cowboys jumped in and out of their saddles many times each day. Large stirrups made the jumping easier and faster.

A cowboy with a poor saddle could fall to the ground and be hurt. A cowboy knew a good saddle was worth more than he paid for it. A good saddle made his work easier and safer.

Detail of a saddle and lasso used at the Douglas Lake Ranch in British Columbia, Canada.

CATTLE DRIVES

Cattle owners wanted the best four-year-old steers, called beeves, taken on a drive because these steers brought the highest price at market. The herd also included cows that could be sold. One- and two-year-old calves were also taken on the drive, to be fattened at the end of the trail before sale, or sold to ranchers who were starting herds in the North. Calves that were born on the trail were killed. Young calves could not keep up with the herd on the trail.

The Chisholm Trail was about 800 miles (1,287 km) long. The Goodnight-Loving Trail was over 1,000 miles (1,609 km) long. Because of the long distances, cattle

owners wanted only the best cowboys to drive their cattle.
The best cowboys brought the most steers to market, and
kept the steers healthy, which meant the cattle owners
made more money.

Cowboys sit on the grass to eat beside their horses and a chuck wagon.

Cattle owners hired about 10 cowboys for a drive. This many cowboys could handle about 2,500 cattle.

Cowboys took few personal things on the drive. Usually, they took a bedroll, a change of clothes, a "slicker" to wear in the rain, a knife, a pistol, and a rifle.

Cattle owners supplied the horses for a drive. This herd of horses was called a remuda. On a typical drive, each cowboy needed about eight horses. The cowboys rotated their horses on the drive so the horses would not get worn out.

Cattle owners also hired a man to take care of the remuda. Cowboys called this man a "horse wrangler." Generally, a horse wrangler cared for about 200 horses.

Every cattle drive had a cook, sometimes called "Cookie." He not only cooked, but also cut hair, sewed clothes, and took care of injuries. He drove the chuck wagon, too.

Charles Goodnight made the first chuck wagon by modifying a U.S. Army wagon. He added a set of drawers to hold flour, lard, coffee, and dried apples. He added a shelf at the wagon's rear that folded down so cooks could prepare food. A chuck wagon carried everything a cook needed.

A trail drive also included one other man: the trail boss. He was in charge of the drive. He rode in front, leading the cowboys and cattle.

Longhorns disliked moving from well-known land to unknown land. To keep them from getting too nervous and starting a stampede, cowboys moved the herd slowly.

A good trail boss knew a herd moved better when it followed a lead steer. Some trail bosses used the same lead steer for several drives. The cowboys also had a leader. The trail boss rode ahead of the cowboys and the herd. He studied the trail, looking for water and grass for the cattle to eat.

Only the most experienced cowboys rode in front of the herd. One rode on the right side, the other on the left. The other cowboys called these men the "point riders."

This cowboy uses a herding dog to help round up the cattle.

Less experienced cowboys rode on each side of the herd. These "swing riders" were about a third of the way back from the point riders.

Other cowboys rode still farther back from the swing riders. "Flank riders" were about two thirds of the way back from the point riders.

The least experienced cowboys rode at the end of the herd, forcing lame, slow, or lazy cattle to keep up. "Drag" or "tail riders" had the worst place in the herd. A herd of 3,000 cattle stirred up a lot of dirt. The drag riders rode in this ever-present dust cloud.

The herd of horses and the chuck wagon followed a good distance behind the herd. The chuck wagon moved ahead of the herd at noon and at supper time.

One eyewitness wrote that a herd he saw was close to one mile (1.6 km) long, and looked like a snake. He wrote that the herd moved about 12 miles (19.3 km) that day.

On the trail, the cook began the cattle drive's day. As the sun rose, he awoke the cowboys. Some cooks yelled, "Grub pile!" Grub pile was slang for a meal that was ready. A cowboy's usual breakfast was sourdough bread and coffee.

After breakfast the cowboys packed their bedrolls in the chuck wagon, then saddled their horses and rode off to round up the herd.

At the herd the point riders guided about 100 cattle away from the night's bed ground. Longhorns disliked moving from their overnight grazing and sleeping land. The point riders slowly and calmly moved them.

Next the swing riders gathered more cattle. They moved them as carefully as the point riders moved theirs. The flank riders gathered more of the herd. They also moved their cattle with care. Finally, the drag riders moved the last of the herd.

In a short time the lead steer and a few older steers moved to the head of the herd. In about an hour the cattle were walking in a long line. They were calm and ready to walk that day's trek, usually about 10 miles (16 km).

After a few days the cattle became "trail broke," and weren't as nervous. Cowboys allowed a trail-broken herd to walk awhile, stop, and graze for a time. While the cattle ate, cowboys kept steers from straying too far from the herd. After the cattle grazed, the cowboys urged them to move again.

At noon the cowboys stopped the herd. The cook had moved the chuck wagon ahead, and had the cowboys' noon meal ready and waiting. Cowboys usually ate sourdough bread, bacon, and beans. On the trail, meat rotted quickly, so good cooks were always searching for extra meat to feed their men. Occasionally, they killed one of the longhorns. However, cattle on a drive had tough meat, so cooks preferred prairie chicken, rabbit, or antelope for extra meat when they could get it.

Cowboys favored a noon stop near water. The herd needed water at least once a day. A watering stop at noon gave the cowboys time to eat and relax, since they didn't need to watch the herd as carefully. Cowboys always let the longhorns drink as much water as they wanted.

On a trail drive, one day was about the same as another. At dawn the cowboys ate. They picked their horses from the remuda, saddled up and rode to the herd. Then they slowly and calmly got the herd moving. At noon they stopped for lunch and a change of horses. Then they moved the herd again until evening.

The cowboys moved the herd about half a mile (.8 km) off the trail at sundown. The trail boss generally found a good place for the night ahead of time. Groups of cowboys took turns watching the herd during the night, working in two-hour shifts. Cowboys hummed or sang to a herd bedded at night.

Herds bedded down for about five hours each night. At about four o'clock the next morning, the cowboys ate breakfast and began another day on the trail.

COW TOWNS

In the spring of 1867, a man named Joseph McCoy traveled by train to Salina, Kansas. The train stopped in a tiny village while a bridge farther up the tracks was repaired. The village, called Abilene, consisted of about 12 log huts, most of which had dirt roofs.

Later, Joe McCoy went back to Abilene. He was looking for a place to ship cattle from. The land around Abilene was excellent pasture land. The Smoky Hill River was nearby. A

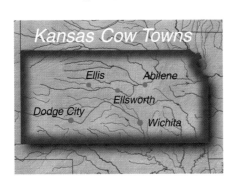

United States Army post, Fort Riley, was also close. Best of all, a railroad went through town.

McCoy bought 250 acres of land near town. On the land he built a stockyard for 3,000 cattle. In town he built a three-story hotel. McCoy then sent a man south to Texas to tell cattle owners to drive their longhorns on the Chisholm Trail to Abilene, Kansas.

But Texas longhorns had small ticks on them. The ticks didn't hurt the longhorns, but they gave milk cows a fever that killed them. Kansas had passed a law in 1861 that banned longhorns from certain parts of Kansas. McCoy made a deal with the governor to get around this law. McCoy agreed to pay for any milk cows that died of the fever. Soon McCoy had a booming cattle business in Abilene.

By the end of 1867, the railroad shipped over 35,000 Texas longhorns from Abilene to Chicago, Illinois. The next year it shipped twice as many. Three years later it shipped 700,000 longhorns to Chicago. Abilene was the first big cow town. In 3 years it went from 12 log huts to a main street with 10 boarding houses, 4 hotels, 5 general stores, and 10 saloons.

But Abilene did not stay a cow town for long. Abilene's citizens had made thousands of dollars from the cattle business, but the cowboys frightened them. After long cattle drives, cowboys were rowdy visitors. They overlooked laws and fought a lot. Because of the cowboys the people of Abilene told the cattle owners to drive their cattle to another town.

Other Kansas towns soon became cow towns. Ellsworth, Wichita, and Ellis served as shipping points for the cattle trade. Dodge City was the last famous Kansas cow town.

Dodge City had once been a center for shipping the hides of the bison, often referred to as the buffalo, back East. But hide prices had fallen, and Dodge City's citizens needed another way to make money. They built stockyards and told longhorn owners to drive their cattle to Dodge City. In 1877, over a quarter of the cattle shipped east on the Santa Fe railroad came from Dodge City.

But the era of the great cattle trade was coming to an end. Settlers were moving to the prairie to claim homesteads and farm the land. The settlers used barbed wire to fence their property and keep cattle from destroying their crops. The great Chisholm Trail was soon broken up by fenced fields. In 1877, Kansas passed a law that banned Texas cattle from the whole state in order to save milk cows from the tick fever. And eventually, railroads built lines into Texas, eliminating the need to drive the cattle north to the railroads in Kansas. By the end of the 1880s, the era of the cowboy had ended on the frontier.

INTERNET SITES

http://www.cowboyhalloffame.org/

Founded in 1965, the National Cowboy Hall of Fame and Western Heritage Center in Oklahoma City, Oklahoma, is a tribute to the men and women who helped establish the West as a part of America's cultural heritage. The site includes a tour of the museum, including the Children's Wing, a special section for kids.

http://www.cowboys.com

Cowboys.com is an electronic shopping mall for products, services, and information for people that have interest in the Western lifestyle. Includes historical information, books, videos, and links to other Western-related Web sites.

These sites are subject to change. Go to your favorite search engine and type in "cowboys" for more sites.

PASS IT ON

History buffs: educate readers around the country by passing on information you've learned about cowboys and cowgirls. Share your little-known facts and interesting stories. We want to hear from you!

To get posted on the ABDO Publishing Company Web site, email us at "History@abdopub.com"

Visit the ABDO Publishing Company Web site at:
www.abdopub.com

GLOSSARY

Bandanna: A handkerchief.

Boarding house: A place where the room rent includes meals.

Chaps: Clothing worn over pants to protect a cowboy's legs. They were usually made of leather. Chaps is pronounced "shaps."

Chuck wagon: A wagon that carries cooking supplies.

Cookie: The cook on a cattle drive.

Cow town: A town from where cattle were shipped east.

Drag rider: Cowboys who rode at the end of a herd.

Farmhands: People who work on farms for pay.

Flank rider: Cowboys who rode on the side of a herd about two thirds of the way back from the front.

Galluses: Another name for suspenders.

Girth: A strap or band that fits around a horse.

Lacquer: A varnish or liquid that hardens after it is put on a surface.

Lead steer: A steer that other cattle naturally follow.

Long johns: One-piece underwear with long arms and legs.

Mustangs: Descendants of the horses that escaped from the Spanish.

Point rider: Cowboy who rode in front of the herd.

Quarter horses: Originally, a mixture of Spanish horses and English horses. The quarter horse has strength, balance, and quick bursts of speed.

Quirt: A small whip.

Remuda: The herd of horses on a cattle drive. A "reserve" herd.

Saddlery: A business that makes or sells saddles.

Skirt: A square piece of leather that spreads out from a saddle.

Slicker: Rain coat.

Stand the gaff: To not run away from hard work.

Stirrups: A ring or frame where a cowboy places his feet.

Sunstroke: A person with sunstroke has high fever and sweats a lot. Sunstroke can make a person pass out.

Swing rider: Cowboys who rode on the side of a herd about one third of the way back from the front.

Tail rider: A cowboy who rode at the end of a herd.

Tick: A small insect that can carry disease.

Trail boss: The man in charge of a cattle drive.

Trail-broke: When cattle are used to moving on a trail.

Warhorses: Horses the Spanish rode in battle.

Wild rag: A bandanna (handkerchief) tied around a cowboy's neck.

INDEX